This Walker book belongs to:

_____

_____

_____

For Rosie — M.J.

For Pippa – never stop exploring — V.W.

The author, illustrator and publisher thank
Dr. Rosie Trevelyan of the Tropical Biology Association
for her help in preparing this book.

First published 2022 by Walker Studio, an imprint of Walker Books Ltd, 87 Vauxhall
Walk, London SE11 5HJ • This edition published 2024 • Text © 2022 Martin
Jenkins • Illustrations © 2022 Vicky White • The right of Martin Jenkins and Vicky
White to be identified as author and illustrator respectively of this work has been
asserted in accordance with the Copyright, Designs and Patents Act 1988 • This
book has been typeset in Helvetica Neue • Printed in China • All rights reserved.
No part of this book may be reproduced, transmitted or stored in an information
retrieval system in any form or by any means, graphic, electronic or mechanical,
including photocopying, taping and recording, without prior written permission
from the publisher. • British Library Cataloguing in Publication Data: a catalogue
record for this book is available from the British Library • ISBN 978-1-5295-1854-2
• www.walkerstudio.com • www.walker.co.uk • 10 9 8 7 6 5 4 3 2 1

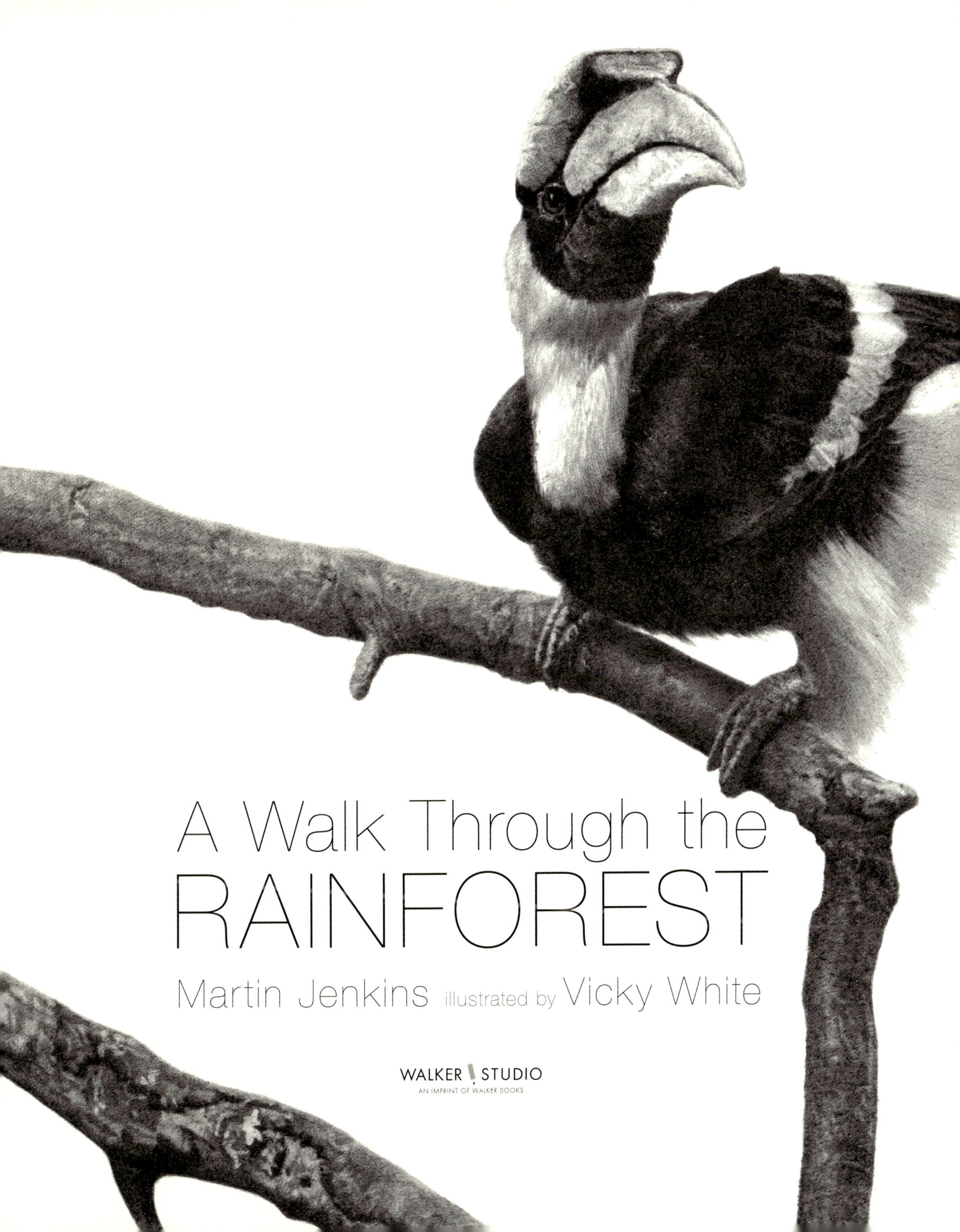

A Walk Through the RAINFOREST

Martin Jenkins illustrated by Vicky White

WALKER STUDIO
AN IMPRINT OF WALKER BOOKS

Tropical rainforests are amazing places. More kinds of animals and plants live in them than anywhere else. This one is in Malaysia in Southeast Asia, in a place called Taman Negara.

Let's go and explore…

What's it like in here? Hot and sticky and pretty dark.

So where are all the animals?

There don't seem to *be* many, apart from a lot of ants and termites scurrying about.

Which is a bit odd when you think that in this forest there are: seven kinds of wild cat; six kinds of pheasant; twelve kinds of pigeon; at least fourteen kinds of squirrel; sixty-six kinds of frog (more or less); eleven kinds of cuckoo; eighty kinds of bat (roughly); ten kinds of owl; nine kinds of hornbill; eighteen kinds of woodpecker; hundreds of kinds of butterfly; goodness knows how many kinds of beetle (I certainly don't), and an awful lot else besides…

Listen for a minute, though.

You may not be able to *see* many kinds of animal but you can *hear* plenty. That whirring is made by cicadas. The loud whistle is a pitta. It's close by but really well hidden. The chattering is a squirrel, though I don't know which kind. And that "woo-woo" is a great argus pheasant, a long way off.

I wonder if it's displaying...

All those animals, all out of sight. But there *are* some wonderful things right in front of us. Can you guess?

It's the trees! They're the biggest things here and the oldest things here. There are loads of different kinds. This one is called a tualang. It must be sixty metres tall and hundreds of years old.

But if you look around carefully, you might notice something a bit odd. The trees here are all big and old. There are no small, young ones. There *are* small plants growing: mosses and ferns, sprawly palms called rattans, wild gingers and arum lilies with dark shiny leaves and strange flowers, but these won't grow into rainforest trees.

Eventually the big trees will die – they could be struck by lightning, or blown down in a storm, or get a disease. But if there aren't any young trees growing around here to take their places, how will the forest keep going?

Let's walk on a while, to see if we can find some clues…

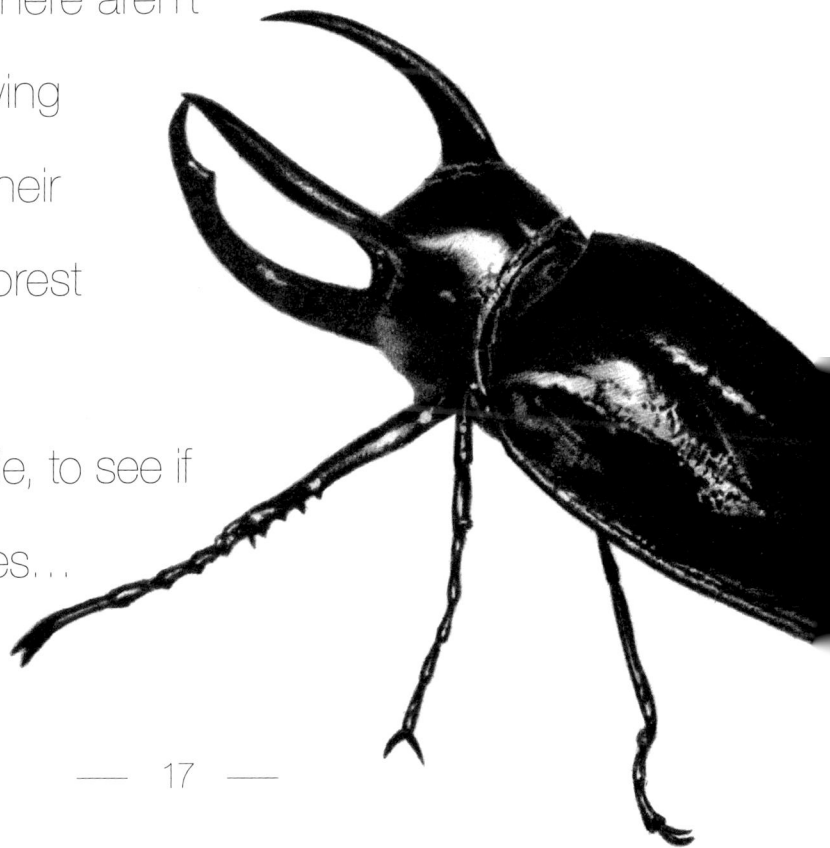

Here's a giant fig tree with lots of fruit on it.

Now we can see some animals! They've all come to feed on the fruit. Those large birds are great hornbills. And there's a family of gibbons too. And some fruit doves. That little bird with a big bill – I think that's a red-crowned barbet. All of them coming to feast.

And there'll be others at night...

And here, under the tree, are lots of fallen figs. There are footprints too, made by wild pigs. They love fruit but have to wait for it to fall to the ground before they can get at it.

Some of the figs have burst open. There are butterflies feeding on the sugary juices. And inside the figs are hundreds of tiny seeds. Any one of those could grow into a giant fig tree if it sprouted. Not here though. It's too dark. Like most forest trees, fig tree seedlings need lots of light to grow well. That's why there aren't any small trees around.

So where *do* they grow?

Let's walk on a little further to see if we can find out.

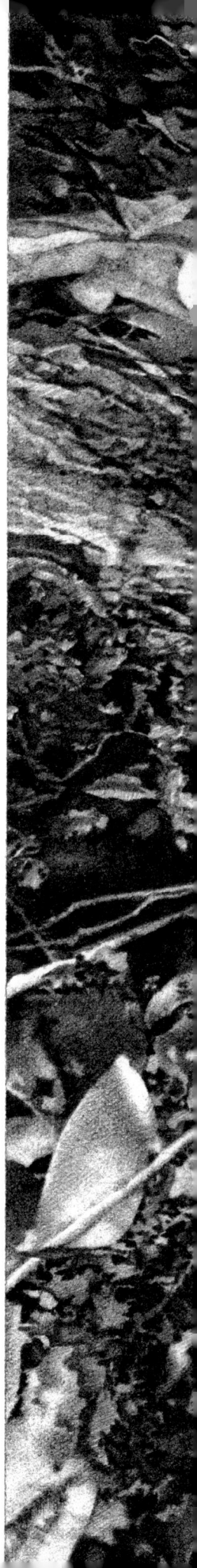

What's this? Some enormous footprints and a big pile of poo. The poo's still warm, which means whatever animal made it was here only recently.

It might be just ahead of us...

It's much lighter here. We've reached a clearing. A huge tree fell in a storm maybe, and pulled down some of the trees around it – their tops would have been all tangled together with vines.

And there are young trees everywhere. *This* is where they grow – in gaps in the forest where sunlight reaches all the way down to the ground.

Each tree grew from a seed. But there aren't any trees with fruit nearby, so how did the seeds get here in the first place?

Look, over there.
Hornbills. They
might be the same
ones we saw at the
fig tree.

Oh. I think one of
them just had a poo.

And here's
another pile of
elephant poo.

And I think that's
wild pig poo.

There's quite a lot
of poo, isn't there?
Let's take a closer
look at some...

The elephant poo is mainly brown stringy stuff – that's the remains of the leaves and branches that the elephant has eaten. But there are also some hard round things. They're durian seeds. Elephants are fond of durian fruit. And if we looked in the pig poo or the hornbill poo, we'd find lots of smaller seeds, like the ones we saw in the figs.

This is how it works: many trees, like figs and durians, make tasty, sugary fruit to attract animals, which eat the fruit along with the seeds. When the animals poo, with luck they'll poo out some seeds and leave them somewhere good to grow.

The poo helps in another way too. Tree seedlings don't just need light, they need chemicals called nutrients which they take up in their roots. Often there aren't many nutrients in rainforest soil, but there's plenty in poo. So when a seed sprouts where an animal has pooed, it should find itself with a supply of nutrients to give it a good start in life.

Of course it's not as simple as that. Some animals, like parrots and squirrels, often chew up and destroy seeds instead of pooing them out whole. Some trees make seeds that are blown about by the wind. They don't need animals to carry their seeds around, so they don't make any tasty fruit. And some trees have seeds that sprout into seedlings that can sit in dark places for years, waiting for the trees above them to fall down to make a clearing.

Whatever kind of seeds a tree makes, hardly any will grow into big trees: they'll rot or get chewed up or end up in bad places to grow. To make up for this, each tree produces huge numbers of seeds. With luck, a few will find themselves somewhere like this clearing, and a few of those will grow into saplings and then into trees. Eventually, in thirty or forty years' time, this won't be a clearing any more...

This happens all the time in the forest. Each of those big trees we saw will eventually die, and a new clearing will open up where it used to stand, waiting for animals that have been feeding on fruit – perhaps from one of the trees that has grown up in this clearing.

And so the forest goes on. And that must be a good thing. Because without the forest there would be nowhere for the seven kinds of wild cat; six kinds of pheasant; twelve kinds of pigeon; at least fourteen kinds of squirrel; sixty-six kinds of frog (more or less); eleven kinds of cuckoo; eighty kinds of bat (roughly); ten kinds of owl; nine kinds of hornbill; eighteen kinds of woodpecker; hundreds of kinds of butterfly; who knows how many kinds of beetle (I certainly don't), and goodness knows what else to live.

And that wouldn't be a good thing at all, would it?

THE WORLD'S RAINFORESTS

Equator

Taman Negara

This map shows the main areas where rainforests grow.

Tropical rainforests are found in parts of the world near the equator where it stays warm all the year round and where there is a lot of rain. There are tropical rainforests in Africa, South and Southeast Asia (like the one in this book), Central and South America, northern Australia, New Guinea, Madagascar and on islands in the South Pacific and the Caribbean.

Tropical rainforests in different parts of the world

look the same, but have different kinds of animals and plants living in them. Nobody knows exactly how many kinds of animals and plants live in tropical rainforests altogether but scientists do know it's an awful lot. They think that between half and two-thirds of all the different kinds that are alive at the moment live in these forests.

People have cut down huge areas of tropical rainforest, mostly to grow crops and keep cattle. This has left all the things that live in rainforests with less and less room. Many of them will die out if we go on cutting down the forests as fast as we are at the moment.

Some rainforests, like the one in this book, are protected in national parks (Taman Negara means "National Park" in the Malaysian language) but not enough of them to make sure that all the living things that need rainforests to survive will be safe.

So many different kinds of animals live in
Taman Negara that we couldn't possibly
fit them all into this book. But we have
put lots in. Did you spot them?

**BLUE-CROWNED
HANGING PARROT**
Loriculus galgulus

BIRDS

GREAT HORNBILL
Buceros bicornis

HOODED PITTA
Pitta sordida

GREAT ARGUS PHEASANT
Argusianus argus

GREAT SLATY WOODPECKER
Mulleripicus pulverulentus

EMERALD DOVE
Chalcophaps indica

BROWN WOOD OWL
Strix leptogrammica

MALAYAN PEACOCK-PHEASANT
Polyplectron malacense

RED-CROWNED BARBET
Psilopogon rafflesii

WHITE-RUMPED SHAMA
Copsychus malabaricus

INSECTS and other INVERTEBRATES

A MILLIPEDE
Class Diplopoda

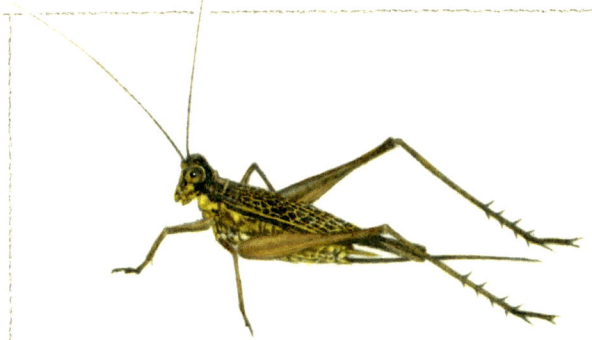

A KATYDID
Family Tettigoniidae

EMPEROR CICADA
Tacua speciosa

GIANT FOREST ANT
Dinomyrmex gigas

TERMITE
Macrotermes carbonarius

ATLAS MOTH
Attacus atlas

EMERALD SWALLOWTAIL
Papilio palinurus

LARGE TREE NYMPH
Idea leuconoe

GREAT MORMON
Papilio memnon

A DUNG BEETLE
Genus Onthophagus

ATLAS BEETLE
Chalcosoma atlas

MAMMALS

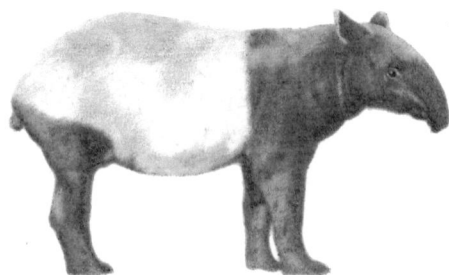

MALAYAN TAPIR
Acrocodia indica

BINTURONG
Arctictis binturong

CLOUDED LEOPARD
Neofelis nebulosa

ASIAN ELEPHANT
Elephas maximus

ASIAN TRI-COLOURED SQUIRREL
Callosciurus prevostii

SUN BEAR
Helarctos malayanus

LAR GIBBON
Hylobates lar

LARGE FLYING FOX
Pteropus vampyrus

SUNDA COLUGO
Galeopterus variegatus

FROGS and REPTILES

BONGAO TREE FROG
Polypedates macrotis

TEMPLE VIPER
Tropidolaemus wagleri

BENGAL MONITOR
Varanus bengalensis

MORE INFORMATION

If you'd like to find out more about tropical rainforests online, the following organisations have good websites:

National Geographic Kids

Rainforest Foundation UK

The World Wide Fund for Nature

World Land Trust

ABOUT THE CREATORS OF THIS BOOK

Both Martin Jenkins' and Vicky White's passion for animals has taken them all over the world – Martin in his work as a conservation biologist, and Vicky in hers as a natural history artist.

This is the third children's book they have created together. Their first, *Ape*, was a winner of the English 4-11 Awards, and their second, *Can We Save the Tiger?*, was shortlisted for the Kate Greenaway Medal.

THESE BOOKS ALSO CELEBRATE
THE NATURAL WORLD:

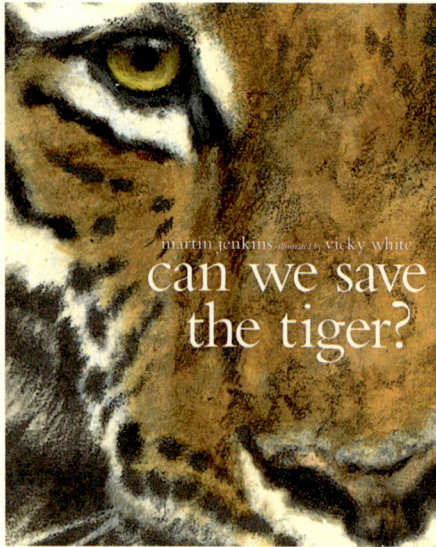

can we save the tiger?

ISBN: 978-1-4063-5638-0

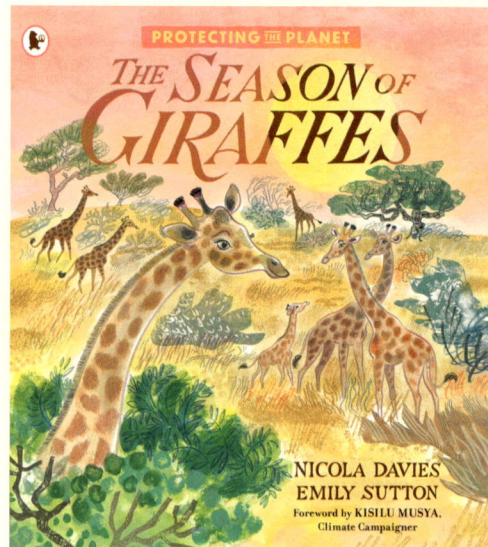

PROTECTING THE PLANET
THE SEASON OF GIRAFFES

NICOLA DAVIES
EMILY SUTTON
Foreword by KISILU MUSYA,
Climate Campaigner

ISBN: 978-1-5295-1392-9

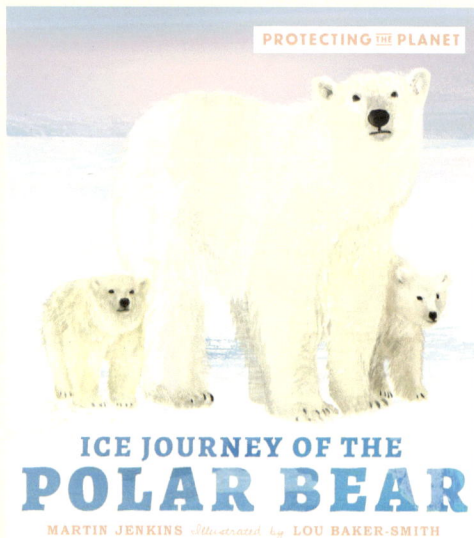

PROTECTING THE PLANET
ICE JOURNEY OF THE
POLAR BEAR
MARTIN JENKINS illustrated by LOU BAKER-SMITH

ISBN: 978-1-5295-0580-1

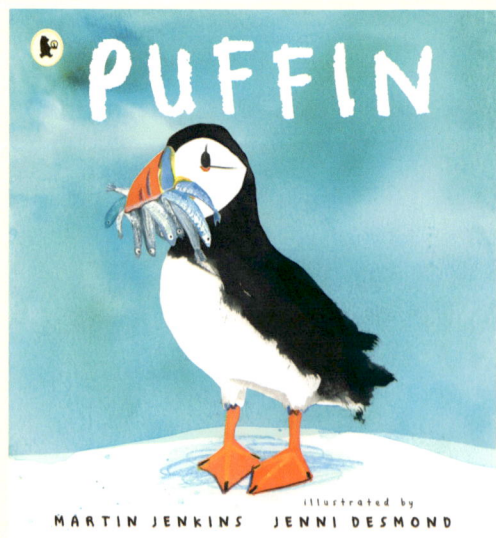

PUFFIN
MARTIN JENKINS illustrated by JENNI DESMOND

ISBN: 978-1-5295-1363-9